LITTLE YOU

Words For Younger "You"

Aeren Laqui

ISBN 978-93-5559-196-8
© Aeren Laqui 2022
Published in India 2022 by Pencil

A brand of
One Point Six Technologies Pvt. Ltd.
123, Building J2, Shram Seva Premises,
Wadala Truck Terminal, Wadala (E)
Mumbai 400037, Maharashtra, INDIA
E connect@thepencilapp.com
W www.thepencilapp.com

Author biography

Aerenis a 20-year-old aspiring novelist from the Philippines who resides in Batangas province. Her father is a regular employee who works hard, and her mother is a loving full-time housewife. She also has a younger sister and an older brother. When she was in sixth grade, she discovered a love for writing. She enjoys writing inspiring short tales, poems, and essays. In sixth grade, she begins participating as a copyreader writer for a journalistic competition. She continues to write, and her work has improved with time. She joins their University Publication Team when she enters university at the age of 18. She went to South Korea as an exchange student at the age of 19 years old. Her nearly seven-month stay in the nation exposed her to the country's cultural diversity and preservation. She returned to her home country of the Philippines and become part of the appointed 2021 Honorary Reporter for the Ministry of Culture, Sports, and Tourism's Korean Culture and Information Service, which aims to promote Korea to the rest of the world through [Korea.net], their official internet platform. She also participated in many domestic and international essay contests that indeed help her to improve her writing skills. Asides from her dream of becoming a Medical Doctor in the future, this young aspiring writer also hopes to publish her book, which will hopefully be an inspiration for others to succeed and be happy, particularly the youth.

CONTENTS

Epigraph

"I wish I had known back then how to enjoy the drizzle or heavy pour of rains."

"I wish I had known back then, being hurt is an emotion that should not be invalidated simply because I am young."

-Little Me

Acknowledgements

Writing a book is more challenging than I expected, but it is also more gratifying than I could have imagined. None of this would have been possible without the people who support and cheer me on every day, from **Kim Desung**(김대성), the first person who ever said I was a good writer. He has never failed to appreciate my writings, which serves as motivation for me to continue.

Aven Silva, Crixia Tisbe, Ren Mendoza, Lowell Manalo, Adrianne Mendoza, Lencie Diane Pasco, Shelley Fae Chan, and Isabella Bathan are among my circle of friends who have been my first critics. It was wonderful to hear that you had nothing except wonderful impressions of me. I'm ecstatic to have you in my life again.

To my family: **Mama Elvie, Papa Louie, Aliya, and Kuya Alvin** for their efforts and encouragement, telling me that I could make this milestone possible.

The visuals I used for this book are all edited in *Canva* to make it more attractive, thanks to them. Finally, I'd like to thank the publishing platform **[Pencil]** that enabled me to publish my first book.

I'd like to express my gratitude to everyone who has ever said anything encouraging to me or taught me something. I heard it all, and it meant something.

ALL THE GLORY AND PRAISE TO YOU, ALMIGHTY GOD!

Introduction

My professor once instructed us in a college class to write a letter to our younger selves. As I write the first line: **"Dear Younger Self,"** it appears to be so simple that I am unable to continue. It's not that I don't have anything to say; in fact, I'm having a lot of ideas that day. It takes me half an hour to get to the next line, and it takes me a long time to assemble all of the words I want to say. When the bell rang, my professor encouraged us to submit our final work. It was at this point that I understood that the toughest aspect of writing a letter to my younger self is not remembering who I was when I was younger and who I am today. The most difficult aspect is recalling an event in my life and realizing, **"I wish I had known these words when I was a teen."** From that day until today, I've gathered my thoughts and chosen to write about things no one else has ever told me about in their lives. Assuming that there is one person in the world right now who has lived as I have in the past and will know what I should have known early on. I aspire that this book will make teenagers or even young adults realized the things I never realized early. **Little You, I wish you know that...**

Little You; YOUR MOTHER IS YOUR BESTFRIEND

When I was a teenager, I used to despise my mother when she scolded me for doing anything wrong. As early as the morning, I became irritated by her voice that leaves me no choice but to get out of my bed. When I don't want to go to school, she becomes angry with me. She also compared me to a child of a neighbor or a relative of ours. I despise the way she described those behaviors as **"discipline"**when I was thirteen years old. I grew up trying hard not to pay attention to what my mother told me till years passed. I've always thought she was simply making up things, and I don't want her comments to ruin my life. That's how I remember my mother; rigid, irritable, and someone I didn't want to be like when I grow up. However, I am wrong. With time, I began to lose everything, which made me realize everything. I began to lose friends, as some of the true ones were preoccupied and had other priorities. I began to enjoy my mother's presence, whether she was happy, sad, or even mad. No matter how long my day is, I always see myself seeking her; she is the first person I look for when I get home. My mother becomes my best friend, someone who I can always count on. She will always be there for me, no matter how hectic her day was. I frequently observe her acting strangely, cracking up with strange jokes, laughing like there's no tomorrow, and even sobbing in the dark. And those are the days when I hated myself much knowing that I could have been there for her a long time ago, but I didn't. I was so self-centered back then that I was oblivious to what my mother was doing for my sake. I'm too deaf to understand that the things she kept repeating to me were meant to comfort me rather than hurt me. It's not when I turned nineteen when she becomes my best friend, she has always been the best friend I didn't notice since I was a child.

Little You,

Your mother will utter a lot of words that may hurt you. But, you may also not realize that your silence harmed them the most. While her actions may make you cry for a short time, they are actions that she will regret for the rest of her life. Her words are not designed to wreak havoc on you; rather, they are meant to strengthen you. The way you treat her frequently makes her question not just her value, but also her responsibility as a mother. I'm sure you understand how much it hurts. Even though she may criticize you a million times, her love for you is uncountable. Appreciate her while you're still young, and as you become older, remember that she's also getting older. Spend time with her to show her how much you care. She is the best person on the planet, and she is well-deserving of the title of friend.

Little You; BEWARE OF YOUR DAD, HE'S A LIAR

When I asked my father for twenty pesos, he always gave me a fifty pesos bill. Whenever I ask him to buy me a burger, he will also purchase me a fried chicken. He once gave me food and asked me to eat it. My first question was, ***"Do you want me to share the meals with you?"*** He responded by saying, ***"No, I already eaten."*** I also recall nearly crying as I was solving a math problem after my father had just returned home from work. I asked him to help me, but my mother said, ***"Your father is tired."*** My father responded, ***"No, I am not tired,"*** and assisted me with my assignment. After asking my father for additional money for the school contribution in 7th grade, I noticed him getting the last 100 pesos bill out of his wallet and he smiled and stated, ***"I still have money left in my other wallet."*** That seemed regular to me at the time. My father, I assumed, was just nice and hardworking. I didn't realize he was a liar until I found out. He intended to save that excess money but whenever I ask for money while I hang out with my friends, he makes sure that I will not get short of it. Whenever he feeds me food, he is also starving but he just wants to make sure that I didn't go hungry. He is fatigued from work every day, but he has never admitted it to me. He only got one wallet, which he has used for the past five years. My dad is a liar, he lied to make sure that we are enjoying a decent life. He lied anytime he stated he's Perfectly all right; for the fact was he is struggling. For our sake, he continues to endure. I should have noticed it sooner rather than later so that my father wouldn't have to bear too much for too long.

Little You,

Unlike your mother, you rarely hear your father talk, yet he is the biggest liar. Keep in mind that his words aren't always reliable. However, he constantly strives to deliver on what he promises. He hides anytime his tears fall, so you won't see him cry. Simply hearing your voice as you greet him good morning, offering him coffee on a rainy afternoon, and even watching you achieve the tiniest things in life make him happy. He is your most secret admirer, and he cheers you on from a distance. To persuade you that he would not be shaken, he attempts to conceal his soft heart. He is, however, sobbing. He may have lied many times, but his love for you is something he can never fake. I hope you can hear the unspoken words your father never wants you to know as early as possible in your childhood.

Little You; YOUR SIBLINGS ARE THE BEST SQAUD

It's difficult to grow up as a middle kid. When I was younger, I felt like an outcast at times. My older brother has a lot of athletic accomplishments, and my little sister is their favorite child. And I, the middle child, will always be the family's **"black sheep."**At the same time, how ironic and sad it is. I recall once telling someone how I hated to tell anybody that I had siblings; how I wished to be the only child so that I would be the center of attention of my parents. I'm always irritated with my brother, and I don't want to share anything with my younger sister. We always say mean things to one another, and I've never been able to win an argument with them. When it comes to them, I believe I will always be the lonely loser. It will not be until I realize that the siblings I hate are the ones who will stick with me through thick and thin. They are the most enjoyable group with whom I can spend my leisure time. Imagine being able to eat for free whenever we go outdoors since my older brother will cover the costs. Imagine getting my younger sister to do the dishes and then watching a movie with her. You know, that's really amusing! But is not all about the free stuff, it's all about the memories you will have with them. It's all about remembering it as you get older. It's all about the challenge you will face altogether and how you will conquer them with each other's support.

Little You,

Don't just spend your days searching for a group of people to hang out with. Sometimes you don't need to look far to find somebody. Sometimes, your lifetime best friends are just a few feet away from you, causing you to be irritated in certain areas of your home. I hope you realize that everyone, even your siblings, has a different love language. It may be difficult to comprehend, but the way your siblings tease you is a sign of their love for you. I hope you don't have to be disappointed that you didn't get to spend more time with them. I hope you realize that, at the end of the day, they are the ones who see your nasty face, which no one of your so-called buddies knows about!

Little You; YOUR CRUSH CAN MAKE YOU CRY

Yes, it's true! When I initially started crying because my crush didn't like me back, I vividly remember the first time. During recess, I genuinely wept like someone had stolen my favorite food. In that period of time, I believed that crying was strange, therefore I would hide in my room anytime I cried. It's funny to remember that I also play sad songs to support my drama. I hate the fact that I am crying because some **"adults"**think that having a crush is not a significant thing. Thus, crying over it makes no sense. I can't tell you how many times I've been upset because my crush had a crush on someone else, but I'll never forget the sorrow I felt at the time. Adults may believe that it isn't painful because I was a child at the time. Perhaps not as sad as adults when their partners cheat on them, but it doesn't negate the fact that it hurts as a child. I hope that I realize early that what I felt before were all "genuine" emotions, the experience of sadness when someone didn't appreciate you. I wish I learned it very early, thus I won't be caught in believing that only grownups may be hurt.

Little You,

Having a crush is a fantastic experience, especially when you're young. Don't be overly concerned about getting your crush's attention. I'm telling you that as time goes on, you'll meet someone who is far preferable to them. It's fine if they ignore you from time to time. Yes, it's pretty fine if you suddenly feel something pinching within your heart. I hope you have the confidence to scream out loud, and don't attempt to hide your emotions. Don't be embarrassed to tell your parents, siblings, and closest friends about it. I'm sure they'll understand you in some way since, like you, they once become a teen. When you're older, you'll laugh at the memories of those tearful moments. However, you may prefer to return to that period, when crying appears to last only a short time.

Little You; LEARNING EXIST EVERYWHERE

As a child, "adults" instilled in me the belief that coming to school every day would help me achieve a bright future. They told me that finishing school was the only path out of poverty for me. Indeed, I may say that it is both wrong and right. As I become mature, I realize that school education is vital since it teaches you skills and information that you may use in your future profession. However, it is not true that you may learn things that will help you find a bright future ***"ONLY IN SCHOOL."*** Learning isn't limited to the classroom; it may be found elsewhere. Things you find by accident, abilities you didn't know you had, issues you'll confront and overcome are all significant experiences that will help you grow as a person. And not only that, there are plenty of things I have acquired in life which have never been taught inside the classroom. I'm still trying to explore and learn at the same time today. It may seem risky to some, but I understand that school is necessary; nonetheless, being able to witness and learn from real life experiences is valuable as well.

Little You,

When your parents encourage you to go to school, listen to them. Pay attention to everything your teacher teaches you, especially in math class. Listen to those who will tell you that school is fun, that it is a place where you may study while also meeting new people. They may claim, however, that only students who excel in mathematics, language arts, music, writing and science would be able to have a bright future— Don't believe them! Don't believe them when they tell you that if you don't have outstanding math grades, you won't be able to become an engineer. You can't be a doctor since you're not excellent at science, don't trust them. Never trust them when they claim that being a teacher is exclusively for people who are brilliant at English. Don't allow such remarks to derail your childhood dreams, though. Please bear in mind that you will need schooling to become a doctor, engineer, or teacher, but that such professions demand characteristics that can be discovered outside of the classroom for the most part. As you study at school, strive to expand your horizons as well.

Little You; ENJOY BEING YOUNG

One of my biggest regrets is that I can't remember a time when I was actually happy as a child. Only the time I'm screaming because I can't open a candy wrapper, the time my mother punished me because I refuse to go to school, and the time my father became sick as a result of being overworked are all I remember. Those are things that make me sad. I can look back and see myself fighting over my siblings, avoiding and missing classes, and plenty of other life events that I don't want to think about anymore. School is where I might meet new people who may have an impact on my life in the future, which is something I wish I had known back then. When I was a child, I wish I had known that arguing with my siblings made no sense; I should have played hide and seek with them. Instead of solving the galaxy puzzle in my room alone, I should have gone out every summer and played with my neighbors During the holidays, I should have made new friends. I often tell myself that if I could turn back time, perhaps I will try my best to at least have a memory that I can genuinely say ***"I am happy!"***

Little You,

Time passed by far too quickly, and you'll no longer be a young child. Now, I hope you learn how to appreciate life and your childhood. During your summer vacations, make new friends and eat your favorite ice cream with them. May you not hate coming to school because of your fearful teachers and bullies. Try to create school buddies that you can share your lunch. I hope you can realize that being a child or a teenager doesn't last for a lengthy time. When you wake up one day, you'll find that you're already a grownup. Believe me when I say that one day you'll want to go back in time and be a child again. But until then, all I hope you can remember are the days when you were happy and enjoying your life as a happy kid.

Little You; FAILURE IS INEVITABLE

Iremember preparing hard for my math exam when I was in high school. I even studied for 2 weeks exclusively for that topic since I know that I am not excellent in mathematics. I really wanted to earn good grades, so I used all of my resources. I study and solves math problems in books, watch mathematics lessons on the internet and even ask my math wizard classmates to offer me hard math questions, I feel certain that I can pass the test, even aspire to perfect it. I'm disappointed as soon as I get the exam paper. The terms used in the test are completely different from what I learned for the last two weeks. Nonetheless, I attempted to answer and solve it, but I just did not know-how. When the bell rang and we were told we had to submit the paper, I knew I was going to fail. As soon as class is over, I begin to wonder why the equations are different, and I struggle to accept that I studied diligently yet ultimately failed. Even if I did my hardest, I loathe myself for being a failure. Since that day, I've always persuaded myself that I'm not good at mathematics and that I won't be able to get excellent marks. I wish I had known early that failure is inevitable, and even if I failed, I should have to keep trying until I succeed.

Little You,

 There will be many moments in your life when you fail because failure is inevitable. Certainly, every failure you face will be terrible and embarrassing, but don't give up. It may be difficult to restart, but there is no harm in trying. I hope you remember that failure will not just occur in your youth; it will also occur as you get older. Train yourself today to deal with the slightest failures you'll have so you'll know how to react as you grow up. You will fail one day, harder than you can imagine, but don't let it discourage you from doing your best.

Little You; LIFE IS TOUGH, BE TOUGHER

It's a rainy afternoon when I went home crying because I forgot to bring an umbrella to school. My uniform and socks are filthy, and tears and rain have covered my face. My mother told me to go into the shower and change my clothing as soon as I entered our house so I wouldn't become sick, so I went to the bathroom, still sobbing. I went straight to my room after that, but I can't stop crying. So, when my younger sister asked as to why I was upset, I simply ignored her. Then I saw a mirror on my table, and when I looked at it closely, I was embarrassed. Actually, I am crying not because I forgot to bring an umbrella and got drenched in the rain, but because a group of schoolboys laughed at me and called me *"a pig"* on the walk home. So, I rushed extremely fast to evade them and suddenly, I fell out the ground and instead of helping me, they simply kept teasing me. I can still imagine myself having no strength to protect myself at that time and just started sobbing. Poor me; if I had realized that it would continually rain heavily in the future, I would have enjoyed the rain more.

Little You,

Life is tough, be tougher! There will be times when you feel hopeless and down. Even if you're still young, you'll feel as if there are always those who will laugh at you when you're at your lowest. You will feel saddened and totally embarrassed but don't be frightened. It doesn't matter how hard it rains that day, how wet you become, how ugly you appear, or how many times you fall to the ground to escape from the taunting people. It doesn't matter how many times you fall and no one takes your hand and makes you stand. What matters is that you're able to continue and bravely walk. I hope that even if you're still young, you'll be able to enjoy the drizzling or even heavy rains that may pour you whenever you forgot to bring an umbrella. Everyone will be teasing you, but I hope you will have the courage to ignore it. I hope you don't expect too much from anyone in hopes of supporting you to stand; I wish you see that you need to get up and mend yourself on your own as soon as possible. When you grow older, you'll see that life has a lot more difficult challenges to give, so be tougher.

Little You; BE KIND TO YOURSELF

"Your acne makes you ugly" "Your nearly gorgeous but you're fat" "Why are you short? At your age?" "White skin fits better on you".These are just some of the words I keep hearing since I was little. And what hurts the most is not the fact that it is repeatedly said to me, but the fact that it is told by my closest relatives. All of my so-called "flaws" are constantly visible in the mirror. I even cried in the bathroom, questioning my worth as a girl. Although I hate taking pictures, I am aware that some other girls my age are attractive, have whiter skin, a slimmer figure, and a beautiful acne-free face. *"I wish I wasn't like this, I want to wake up pretty like them,"*I remember praying one time. I always envy my friends who are called "gorgeous" by others. People were pushing me to try different types of diets when I was nine years old. At the age of 10, I kept browsing on the internet about what face products I may use to get rid of my acne. When I understood I needed to embrace who I am, I was already a grownup. I should have walked confidently through the school corridor if I had realized it sooner. I shouldn't have worn jackets amid the summer to hide my flabby body. I shouldn't have learned to use make-up to conceal my acne before reaching 18 years old. If I can only go back, I will never permit anyone to call me "ugly" just because I cannot reach their "so-called" ideal of beauty.

Little You,

Make it a habit to start with yourself always. Do what you desire, abandon what you hate. In your youthful days, I hope you discover that it's acceptable to pursue a different road. Please find the courage to refuse and disregard comments that will one day kill your enthusiasm and confidence in anything else. Because you are not forced to fit into someone's shoes, be fair to yourself. You do not belong to someone's high hopes and expectations. Early today, may you understand that you have your own prose and poetry. You are entitled to loathe yourself on occasion, but you are also permitted to admire your curves and flaws. Even if the world tells you otherwise, you are lovely and worthwhile.

MY CHILDHOOD POETRY

I started writing poems when I was in 2nd grade. I'm thankful that one Sunday morning while cleaning my closet, I discovered a notebook containing some of the poems I wrote as a child. I decided to also put some of my favorite pieces and acknowledge my younger self for her good work.

-Author

CANDY WRAPPER

Whose candy is that? I think I know.
Its owner is quite sad though.
It really is a tale of woe,
I watch her frown. I cry hello.

She saw the words ***"TEAR HERE"***,
And sobs until the tears make.
The only other sound's the break,
Of distant waves and birds awake.

The candy wrapper is hard to open, slippery and thin
But she has promises to keep,
Until then, she shall not sleep.
With thoughts of sadness on her distress.

BIRDS AND FISH

Birds flew freely in the sky
Go everywhere side to side
Flaps its feather and go around
Go to tress and rest a while

Fish swim freely under the sea
See the world green and blue
Wave their fin side to side
Hide to corals and rest a while

If suddenly the bird wanders around
Stand in a floating stone at sea
The fish jump and saw her beauty
The bird was stunned to move

They loved each other at first sight
Will they be meeting the next time?
If that so happened how could it be?

Can fish and birds have a home where together they can live?

WINTER

What if it snows in a tropical country like this
I might build a snowball and go for a fight
What if the snow falls from the cloud
I won't run as fast, unlike when it rains
What if I can see the snow for the first time
I would like to know how it tastes when it lands
If there's snow and it's snowing hard, will I be drowned?

HAIRPIN

I look at the mirror I see myself
Smiling, laughing, but you know what else?
I am not that happy these past few days
I keep searching for my pink hairpin

I search for it everywhere in the room
Under the bed, chair, and books
I found nothing but a nasty dust
I just sneeze and cough aloud

I found an old glass on the sides
Due to carelessness, it fell to the ground
It broke into pieces and, there's my reflection appears
I saw the hairpin I struggled to find

All the time, it's just been there
In my hair, the pin I used to wear
Why should I search far and wide?
If it is just in the right place all the time

TO OLDER ME

May you not hate remembering me
For I am such a crybaby
May you not deny that I too, once exist
Inside your heart, hope there's still a place for me

I have so many insecurities
I also have uncertainties
I can't speak confidently
Those are things you may hate about me

I always cried questioning my worth
Asking why I feel not okay
When the world sleep at 3am
Here I am in silence wishing, to have some rest

In this sadness, there's a promise I will keep
Every morning, I still choose to breath
I will carry the burden day by day
So one day, I can see— you too will exist.

XIX

It feels like yesterday I am just seven

However today— it's the start of my last year of being a teen

Yet, some things aren't change

I stil cry when I couldn't open a candy wrapper just like I was four

I still do write poetries that started since I was on my 2nd grade

The difference is just, I used to write for others however now—

I do write for myself and it feels much satisfying, appreciated and better.

XIX
Nineteen

GRATEFUL (감사하다)

For the strange streets we've walked
(우리가 걸어온 낯선 거리를 위해)
Strangers turn into friends we've met
(낯선 사람은 우리가 만난 친구로 변한다.)
Sadness we've conquer
(우리가 극복한 슬픔)
Pledges we kept
(우리가 지킨 공약들)

For the pain
(통증을 위해)
Unreciprocated love
(짝사랑)
Fears we've hide
(우리가 숨긴 두려움)
Memories that haunt us
(우리를 괴롭히는 기억들)
And the little hope that's left
(그리고 남은 작은 희망은)

For the victories we celebrated
(우리가 축하한 승리를 위하여)
Tears we wiped

(우리가 닦아낸 눈물)
And wounds left by failures
(그리고 실패가 남긴 상처는)

Every little things we experienced
(우리가 경험했던 모든 작은 것들)
In this year taught us to be tougher
(올해에는 우리에게 더 강해지라고 가르쳤다)
And prouder and better
(그리고 더 뿌듯하고 더 좋다)
And genuinely braver
(그리고 정말 용감해)

For another year we're going to face
(앞으로 1년 동안 우리는 마주하게 될 것이다)
May we got sparkles that will never fade
(영원히 사라지지 않는 반짝임이 우리에게 있기)
Strenght that will never buckle
(절대 버클이 채워지지 않는 힘)
Faith that will remains unswayed
(흔들리지 않는 믿음)
In this world full of discouragement
(낙담으로 가득찬 세상에서)
Prayer will always going to be our defense
(기도는 항상 우리의 방어일 것이다)

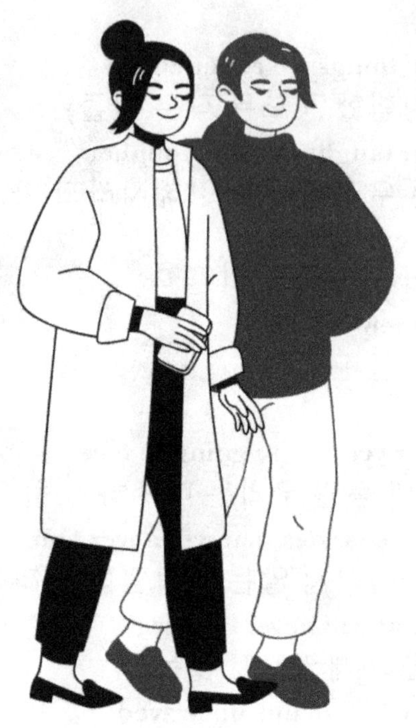

WORDS FOR YOU

MY CHILDHOOD WAS NEVER PERFECT, BUT I WANT THE READER TO KNOW THE THINGS I NEVER REGRETTED AS A CHILD, AND I HOPE THAT AFTER READING THIS CHAPTER, YOU WILL BE ABLE TO EMBRACE AND NOT BLAME YOUR YOUNGER SELF FOR WHO YOU HAVE BECOME.

-AUTHOR

BEING A WRITER

If there's one thing I'll never regret doing as a child, it was aspiring to be a writer. I always write no matter what I feel, I always have an updated journal and diary about my day. Because writing has become my escape, I never skip writing. At an early age, I began writing poems, essays, and even songs. Some once told me that writing is hard since you need to have decent grammar and firm thinking. However, I believe they are mistaken. To be a writer doesn't need to become competent in any foreign language, and is too detailed about the grammatical structure. You only need to have an emotion and a desire to be a writer. How a person uses her words to reach the mind and hearts of her readers is what makes her create a wonderful masterpiece, not how she uses them. Certainly, my passion for words created who I am today— **stronger and better.**

BEING A GOOD FRIEND

Ican't deny the truth that as I grew older, I have lost a lot of friends. My circle shrinks much more than it did when I was a teenager. However, being a good friend is something I would never regret. I once begged a friend to stay in my life, and I still don't regret it. My best friend once betrayed me, yet I never hold anything against her. I feel sad whenever I realized that some of my friends have the power to replace me anytime and easily, but I am still pleased that I once met them. It doesn't matter to me whether they are good friends or not; what matters is that I have been and will always be a good friend to them. It's never been easy to stay a good friend even after some of your so-called "friends" turn their back on you, but I guess it taught me how to be brave. It takes a lot of courage to accept that some people are only meant to stay for a while. It takes a brave heart to accept that some friendship doesn't really exist. For that, I am proud of my younger self. I am proud because she manages to endure how frustrating and painful it is. Until today, I owe my younger self for always choosing to be a good friend.

www.ingramcontent.com/pod-product-compliance
Lightning Source LLC
LaVergne TN
LVHW050327051125
825063LV00045B/1478